When I Go to Church

by Kay Vandevier Henry

Guiding Preschoolers in Worship REVISED

M000007498

This book belongs to:

Josie Ann Lovett

(Your Name)

Illustrated by **T. F. Cook**

Dedication

With love to my parents, Joseph E and Virginia (DeSilver) Vandevier,

who guided me in my first worship experiences.

© Copyright 2011 LifeWay Press®

All rights reserved

No part of this work may be reproduced or transmitted in any form or by any means, electronic or mechanical, including photocopying and recording, or by any information storage or retrieval system, except as my be expressly permitted in writing by the publisher. Requests for permission should be addressed in writing to LifeWay Press®, One LifeWay Plaza, Nashville, TN 37234-0172

ISBN: 9-7814-1587-0464

Item Number: 005397465

Dewey Decimal Classification Number: 268.432

Subject Heading: DISCIPLESHIP TRAINING–PRESCHOOLERS

Printed in the United States of America

Childhood Ministry Publishing

LifeWay Church Resources

One LifeWay Plaza

Nashville, TN 37234-0172

All Scripture quotations are taken from the Holman Christian Standard Bible®, copyright 1999, 2000, 2002, 2003, 2009 by Holman Bible Publishers. Used by permission.

How to Use this Book

- Personalize this book for your older preschooler by helping him write his name on the title page. When you read a story to him, substitute his name in place of the main character's name.

- Use the stories as springboards for discussing new experiences with your child and preparing him for congregational worship. Consider using the names of your family and friends in adapting a story to your own situation and church environment.

- Underline insights as you read the pages of guidance for parents interspersed throughout the book. Perhaps your church can present a copy of this book as a gift to families. As an alternative, several copies could be placed in the church media center or library for parents to check out.

- Encourage church leaders to read this book. Worship leaders in your church may find the guidance segments helpful in encouraging other adult worshipers to welcome older preschoolers to the service. Church leaders who model acceptance and understanding of preschoolers in worship services are following Christ's instruction, "Whoever welcomes one child … in My name welcomes Me" (Matthew 18:5).

- Use this book as a resource for conducting a conference for parents and church leaders. Refer to pages 48-50 for a conference plan with discussion questions and training insights. Or jot down your responses as you use the discussion questions as a personal study guide.

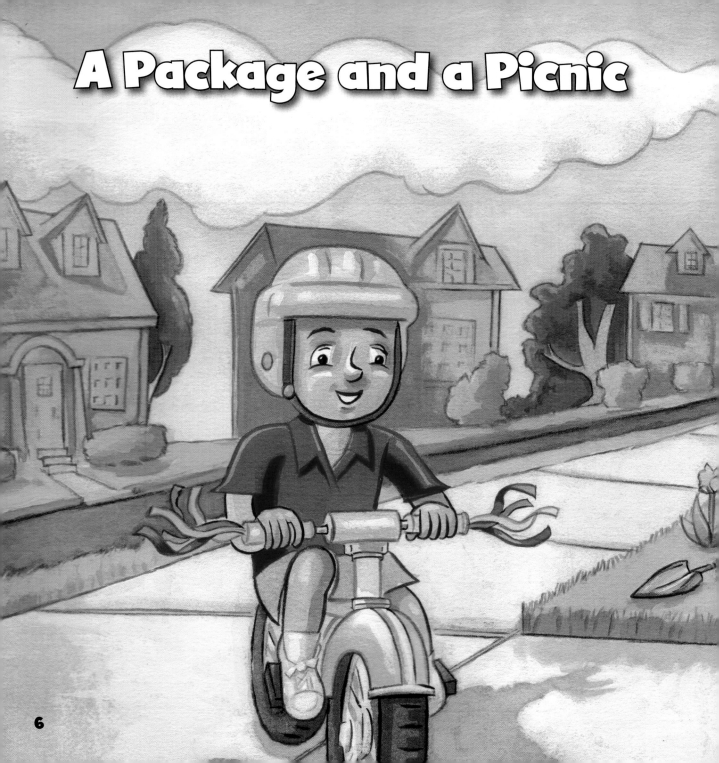

A Package and a Picnic

Vroom—vruum—vroom. Round and round went the bicycle wheels, and faster and faster went Zachary's legs. "It's a pretty day for a picnic," Zachary sang.

Sidewalk to house. House to sidewalk. The bicycle went faster and faster up and down the sidewalk.

Screeeeech. Suddenly, Zachary stopped. A man was walking on the sidewalk. He was carrying a big bag of letters and packages.

"Mother! Look! The mail is here," Zachary shouted.

Mother removed her gardening gloves and took a package from the mail carrier. "Thank you. Have a nice day," she told the man.

"Surprise, surprise, Zachary! The package is for you. Come look," Mother said.

Zachary held the package. It was heavy.

"What's in my package, Mom?"

"Come with me inside the house and you can open it," she said.

Zachary and Mom sat in the kitchen table. Rip—zip—rip. Off came the paper. Zachary opened the box. Inside was a book with a picture of Jesus on it.

Mother picked up a note that fell to the floor. She read: "This Bible is for a big boy who is old enough to go to big church. Love, Grandpa Kelly."

Carefully Zachary turned the pages in the bright new Bible. "Look at all the pictures, Mom. I love my new Bible!"

Just then the kitchen door opened, and Daddy and Katelyn came in. They looked at the new Bible. "I found a picture of Baby Jesus!" Katelyn exclaimed.

Then inside the house Mother said, "All of you can help pack the picnic lunch while I make the sandwiches."

Zachary helped Daddy and Katelyn put everything in a box. First, they packed the tablecloth, paper plates, napkins, cups, and plastic forks and spoons.

Next, they added the potato salad, hardboiled eggs, bananas, cookies, and lemonade. Then mother packed the sandwiches.

Zachary placed his new Bible on top of the picnic box. On the drive to the park, Zachary opened and looked at his Bible. He liked the shiny picture pages.

"Let's unpack and eat," Daddy said as he parked near a shady picnic table.

Zachary laid his Bible beside his car seat before he jumped out to help.

When everything was ready, Daddy said, "Let's thank God." Mother, Daddy, and Katelyn each said a prayer. They thanked God for food, happy times, sunshine, and shady trees.

Then it was Zachary's turn. "Thank You, God, for Grandpa Kelly. And thank You for my new Bible."

After lunch, Mother rested on a blanket under a tree. She watched everyone play with a big beach ball.

Whack—whick—whack. "Higher, higher!" Zachary shouted. Even when the ball went as high as the trees, Zachary could catch it.

The sky was turning dark when Daddy drove home. "Time for baths and our quiet time," Mother said as they went inside the house.

"I'll help unpack the picnic box," Daddy said. "Katelyn, please help Zachary run his bath water."

Everyone helped. After his bath, Zachary looked in his closet. "Which clothes will I wear tomorrow?" he wondered. "Mom, will you help me choose my Sunday clothes?" Zachary called.

Zachary and Mother laid out brown slacks, a green shirt, and brown shoes. Beside his clothes, Zachary laid his new Bible. Everything was ready for Sunday.

"Let's have our quiet time in my room tonight," Zachary suggested.

"Okay," Mother said. "Will you let us read from your new Bible, Zachary?"

"Yes, and I will turn the pages," Zachary offered. When everyone found a place to sit, Daddy helped Zachary open his Bible to Luke, chapter 2.

Daddy read several verses, and then he said: "Luke 2:27 tells us that Jesus went to church with His family. After Sunday School tomorrow, Zachary, you will go to worship

service with us. I'm glad you are growing bigger and can sit with us."

Then Daddy prayed: "Thank You, God, for our family. Thank You for our church and for the Bible."

After a goodnight kiss from everyone, Zachary snuggled into his cozy bed. "Thank You, God, for surprises," Zachary whispered. "And thank You for helping me grow big enough to sit with Mom and Dad in church tomorrow."

Choosing and Using a Bible

You have the privilege of helping your child become aware that the Bible is a special book that helps people learn about God. As your child handles and uses her own Bible, she can begin to associate the Bible with feelings of enjoyment, discovery, acceptance, and love.

- Choose a Bible appropriate for her age. The Read to Me Bible for Kids[1] is a wonderful choice and contains colorful, realistic pictures; suggested Bible verses and stories; and information on age-appropriate biblical concepts and skills.
- Print your child's name in the Bible.
- Look at pictures and talk about verses and stories.
- Make up simple songs about Bible friends (use familiar tunes).
- Help your child make Bible markers from construction paper, yarn, or ribbon.
- Encourage your child to use her Bible in worship services.
- Be a role model for your child as you read, study, and use your own Bible at home.

Worship Begins in the Home

Preschoolers learn to worship God from family members who show love for God as they rest, dress, eat, travel, and engage in other daily routines (Deuteronomy 6:7). Consider the following as opportunities for worshipful moments:

- Encourage your child to say a thank-you prayer at mealtime (or anytime).
- Thank God for the beauty you and your child enjoy outside. Talk about the color of the blue sky, the smell of a honeysuckle bush, or the splash of rain.
- Sing simple songs such as "Mary has two eyes to see, eyes to see, eyes to see. / Mary has two eyes to see. / Thank You, God" (tune "Mary Had a Little Lamb").
- Involve your child in family devotion times by encouraging her to hold the Bible, sing a song, or say a prayer.

---

[1]This Bible, available in KJV (001011446) and HCSB (005034982), may be purchased from LifeWay Christian Resources by calling 1 (800) 458-2772, by ordering online at *www.lifeway.com,* or by visiting your nearest LifeWay Christian Store.

Getting Ready for Church

You set the stage at home for your child's good experiences during a Sunday worship service. Your positive conversation about God, prayers at mealtimes, and reading the Bible together are important ways to worship God in your home.

In addition to these daily actions, make specific plans on Saturday to prepare your child ahead of time for your worship experience.

• Talk to your child as you anticipate Sunday's worship service. Say: "I'm glad you will sit with me during the worship service tomorrow, Christopher." Or "Tomorrow is a special day. We are going to church."

• Explain various aspects of the church service, such as the greeting of visitors, offering time, and special music segments. You might say, "Giving our offering is one way we worship God."

• Make sure your child gets enough sleep on Saturday night.

The night before is a good time to make decisions about clothes to wear. For example, selecting clothes for Sunday on Saturday night not only saves time, but also allows you to help your child begin to anticipate Sunday's activities. Church services are more likely to be a time of celebration and worship when you get ready in these ways:

• Get up early so your family is not rushed.

• Start the day with a prayer for your family and your church.

• Provide a nourishing breakfast.

• Share tasks so everyone helps with getting ready.

• Stay calm and pleasant.

• Enjoy travel time to church as an opportunity for positive, loving conversation.

Veronica's Special Visit to Church

"I see it! I see it!" Veronica shouted and pointed.

Grandmother Gonzalez and Veronica walked beside their apartment building.

They were making a special visit to the big church across the street.

"Yes, that is the steeple," said Grandmother.

"I see the tall, tall church steeple," Veronica said. She took little skipping steps, slippity—slappity—slippity. She was excited because today she was going to see the place for worship inside the church.

"On Sunday evening you'll sit with your Daddy during the worship service," Grandmother said. "You're getting to be

a big girl, and it's time for you to sit in church with us."

Veronica and Grandmother walked up the steps into the church. Veronica helped open the big doors. They walked through a wide, tall hallway.

"Big, big, big," whispered Veronica. She and Grandmother walked on the soft red carpet to the back row of seats. "And I see zillions of these special church chairs," Veronica said.

Grandmother and Veronica sat down on the soft, padded chairs.

Grandmother began to sing softly, "Yes, Jesus loves me, The Bible tells me so." Veronica helped Grandmother sing the song.

"Come walk with me to the front of the worship center," Grandmother said. Veronica saw rows and rows of more chairs—more than she could count. She saw big lights on the tall ceiling.

The red carpet stretched a long way. At the front of the worship center, Veronica saw many things, and she asked many questions.

"Let's play a game," Grandmother suggested. "Let's walk around and when you touch something you want to know about, I'll answer your questions."

Offering plate, pulpit, microphone, music stand, piano, balcony steps, stained glass window. Veronica touched things, and Grandmother answered her questions.

She touched shiny wood, cool metal, and soft cloth. She and Grandmother talked about beautiful colors, tall spaces, and special places in the worship center.

They were still talking about the beautiful things when Mr. Bill came in.

"Hi, Veronica. Hi, Mrs. Gonzalez," Mr. Bill said. Veronica was glad to see Mr. Bill.

"I know Mr. Bill," she told Grandmother. "He sings songs. Sometimes he plays his guitar in my Sunday School room."

"I have my guitar with me. Would you like to sing with me now?" Mr. Bill asked.

Thrum—strum—thrum. Veronica sat beside Mr. Bill and Grandmother, and they sang softly. Veronica liked being in the worship center with the sounds, colors, and special things. "Thank you, Mr. Bill," she said.

"Veronica, it's time for us to visit with Mrs. Fry," Grandmother said. "She has a surprise for you!" Veronica and Grandmother walked through the long halls to Mrs. Fry's office. Mrs. Fry had a small, shiny sign on her desk.

"Hello, Mrs. Fry. What does your sign say?" Veronica asked.

"The words on the sign are Children's Minister," Mrs. Fry replied.

"I know that you are a church helper," Veronica said. "You help boys and girls at church."

"Yes, I do help children at church," Mrs. Fry said. "And I want to give you a copy of a special book about going to worship service. Your dad can read the stories to you." Veronica looked at the pictures in her new book while Grandmother and Mrs. Fry talked.

"I love my new church book!" Veronica said. "It is an awesome surprise. Thanks, Mrs. Fry."

As Veronica and Grandmother walked home, Veronica held on tightly to her new book. She could hardly wait to show it to Daddy. She was excited that she would be going to worship service soon. The worship center was big, but it was a special place.

"I'm big now," Veronica sang as she took little slippity—slappity—slippity skipping steps beside Grandmother. "I'm big enough to go to worship service with my daddy!"

What Is Worship to a Child?

To a preschooler, worship may mean:

• the place where the pastor preaches;

• an activity that only adults can enjoy;

• a long time to sit still and be quiet;

• the negative correction from adults for talking and fidgeting.

A preschooler's negative experiences may block the development of positive attitudes toward worshiping God. Since the attitudes formed early in life may impact the rest of life, the hope of parents and of church leaders is for preschoolers to see worship as the following:

• a special place where everyone, including children, can enjoy the color, movement, music, beauty, and awe of worshiping God;

• the special actions of singing, praying, giving, reading the Bible, and learning about Jesus;

• a special time to be with family and friends who love God;

• the positive feelings of belonging, loving, giving, and sharing.

How can the adults make worship meaningful to children? The following actions are important:

• Pay attention to children. Greet preschoolers and call them by name.

• Acknowledge the need of preschoolers to move around and make some noise. Ignore small distractions.

• Recognize publicly the presence and participation of children in the service. Involve older children from time to time in reading a Scripture, handing out bulletins, or greeting people.

• Embrace the fact that the spiritual nurture of children is a responsibility of the entire church.

Jesus indicated that children are important (Mark 10:13-16). Jesus gave His love and attention to children. Churches should not neglect the nurture of young children—by design or default—as participants in the community of worshipers.

Visiting the Worship Center

Take time to help your child explore the worship center. A brief tour will give you the opportunity to explain aspects of the worship service and answer questions.

- Call your church office to arrange a time when you and your child can visit.
- Keep the visit informal and comfortable for just the two of you.
- Recognize that your child's curiosity and desire to explore will prompt her to touch items.
- Sit together in a pew or seat. Sing a song, talk about stained glass windows or other decorations, or pray together.
- Walk to the pulpit or praise team area. Explain new words such as pulpit, platform, microphone, and music stand.
- Recognize that positive experiences may help your child develop important lifelong responses to worship services such as a sense of belonging, the desire to participate, and joy in worshiping.

Getting to Know Church Helpers

Church helpers, both volunteer leaders and the church staff, often become important role models for preschoolers.

Provide opportunities for your child to meet the ministers, musicians, secretaries, custodians, deacons, and other church leaders. Help your child greet these friends with a smile and handshake.

- Arrange a time for you and your child to visit briefly with church staff members in their offices during the week.
- Talk about church helpers and what they do at church and during worship services.
- Enlist your child's help in mailing birthday or special occasion cards to church helpers.
- Recognize that positive relationships at church may help your child develop the attitude: "I rejoiced with those who said to me, 'Let us go to the house of the Lord'" (Psalm 122:1).

Zachary's First Worship Service

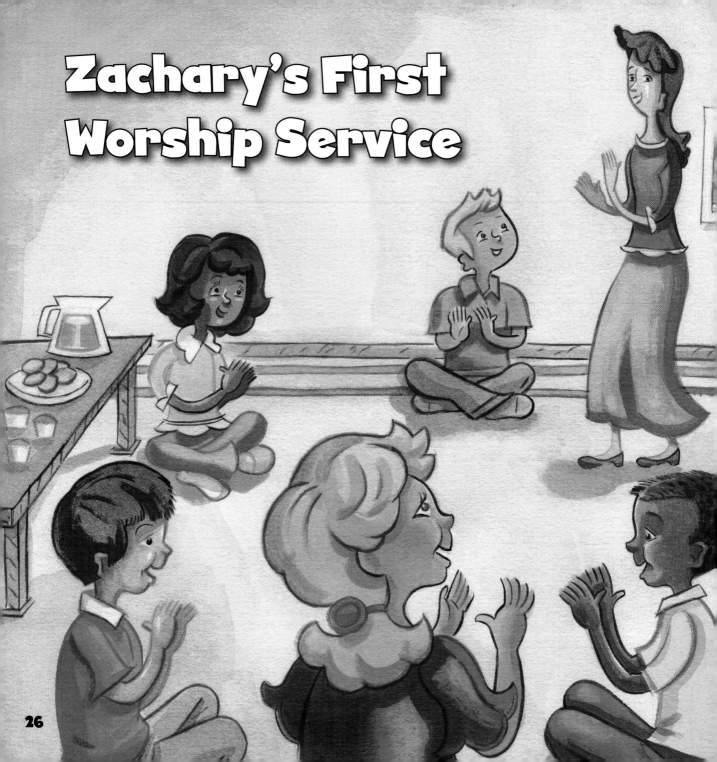

"**I**f you're happy and you know it, clap your hands," Zachary sang loudly with the boys and girls.

"Your daddy is here," Mrs. Wong whispered in Zachary's ear. Zachary quickly left the Sunday School group time and walked to the door.

"Here are your picture and Bible," Mrs. Wong said. "I hope you enjoy the worship service, Zachary."

Daddy helped Zachary put the finger-painting picture in a paper bag. "I'll carry your picture in this bag, and you can carry your Bible to the worship service," Daddy told Zachary.

Daddy and Zachary walked down a long hallway. "Hi, Mr. Neal. I'm going to worship service today," Zachary called out as they passed one of Daddy's friends.

"We need to make two stops before we meet Mom and Katelyn in the worship center," Daddy said. "Here are the restrooms and the drinking fountain, Zachary."

Soon Zachary and Daddy were ready to go to the worship service. At the door, Mr. and Mrs. Howard gave Zachary a bulletin. "Thanks, Mr. Howard," Zachary said. "I'll let my daddy read this church paper, too. We'll share."

Daddy and Zachary stood inside the doors at the back of the church. "Let's listen to the music for a minute while we look for Mother and Katelyn," Daddy said. "Katelyn has a surprise for you later."

Soon Zachary and Daddy saw Mother

and Katelyn sitting in a pew close to the front. As Zachary walked down the aisle,
he waved to his friend, Alexander.

"Zachary, you can sit here at the end of the pew beside me," Daddy said quietly
as they sat down.

"I'm glad you're here, Zachary," Mother whispered as she smiled and winked.

Just then the music got louder. People stood and began singing the words, "This
is the day that the Lord has made."

"The worship service is beginning," Zachary whispered to Daddy.

Daddy squeezed Zachary's hand. "I'll help you know what to do," Daddy said.

Zachary stood as tall as he could beside Daddy. He sang loudly. Clap—clap—clap! When Daddy clapped his hands, Zachary clapped, too.

After the music, Pastor Gates said: "We want to welcome anyone who is visiting our church. Would you please raise your hand if you are visiting?" Zachary saw 1-2-3-4 people raise their hands.

People began shaking hands. "It's good to see you in worship service, Zachary," said Mr. Neal as he shook Zachary's hand.

When the people sat down, Pastor Gates said: "A young lady will help us by reading the Scripture today. Katelyn, please come read the Bible for us."

Surprise, surprise! Zachary's sister was helping Pastor Gates today! Katelyn walked to the pulpit, opened her Bible, and read from it.

"Katelyn is a church helper!" Zachary whispered to Daddy.

"And you're a church helper, too, when you listen and pray and sing," Daddy said softly as he patted Zachary's arm. Zachary sat up tall in his pew seat when Katelyn sat beside him.

After Pastor Gates said a prayer, Zachary watched as men passed offering plates down the pews.

"It's time for you to give your offering," Daddy whispered to Zachary. Plink—plunk—plink. Zachary quietly dropped 1-2-3 quarters into the offering plate.

When Pastor Gates began preaching, Daddy gave Zachary paper and a pencil. Scritchy—scratchy—scritchy. The pencil made small noises as Zachary drew pictures of the church. He heard Pastor Gates talking about loving your neighbors, so Zachary drew a picture of the Riley family who lived next door to his house.

Just then, everyone stood and began singing again. Several people walked to the front of the church and talked with Pastor Gates and shook his hand.

After a prayer, the worship service was over. People were talking and laughing together. "Let's go shake Pastor Gates' hand," Daddy told Zachary.

"I'm glad to see you here," the pastor said. He shook Zachary's hand. Zachary felt special.

It was time to go home, and it was time for lunch. "Thank You, God, for a happy surprise at church," Zachary sang softly. He sang louder as he walked to the car with Mother, Daddy, and Katelyn. "Happy, happy day!" he sang.

Setting the Stage for Worship

Before you take your child into worship service, plan time for the following:

- Take her to the restroom.
- Stop at a water fountain so she can get a drink.
- Store any Sunday School art or nature projects in a paper or plastic bag.
- Thank God for the blessing of worshiping with your child.

Take a moment to greet church friends on the way to the worship center. Include your child in the conversation. You might say: "Mrs. Holt, this is my daughter, Emily. We are happy that Emily is coming to worship service with us."

To further help your child feel involved, encourage her to:

- shake hands with church friends;
- open the door to the worship center;
- get a copy of the church bulletin;
- carry and use her own Bible;
- give an offering.

Remember to provide your child with money at the appropriate time during the service. Paper bills are easier to retrieve if accidently dropped, but many preschoolers enjoy the weight, number, and noise of dropping coins into an offering plate.

Arrive early enough to find a seat close to the front at the end of a center aisle where your preschooler can see. If your church has a balcony, this may be a good choice for seating. When preschoolers cannot see what is happening, they become bored, move where they can see, or climb on the pews for a better view. By choosing the right seat, you may be able to avoid these problems.

Guiding Behavior During the Worship Service—Part 1

Although a young child may not understand all of the words, symbols, and actions of congregational worship, he can begin to sense the importance of worship. Your positive guidance and encouragement will assist him as he participates in these ways:

- He can sit, stand, pray, and sing at appropriate times. Gently prompt his involvement. If songbooks are used, "underline" the words with your finger so he can follow along.
- He can greet people and shake hands. Model this and include him in greetings.
- He can bring and use a Bible. Help him find the sermon Scripture in his Bible.
- He can give an offering and help pass the offering plate. Prepare and guide him with this.
- He can listen to announcements, testimonies, and the sermon. Point out these items in the bulletin.
- He can observe and follow the example of his family and other worshipers.
- He can observe and enjoy the rich colors, architectural forms, and beauty of the worship center.
- He can use paper and pencil or crayons to draw. You might suggest that he draw something the pastor says or something he sees in church. Or, you could ask him to listen for words like *Jesus* or *Bible* and then make a mark on his paper.
- He can ask you questions quietly. You can whisper brief guidance.
- He can enjoy closeness by leaning against you, standing beside you, sitting on your lap, or holding your hand.

Following the service, thank your child for the specific ways he participated.

Scrubbity—rubbity—scrubbity.
Veronica washed her hands with soap
and water.

Splishy—splashy—splishy.
Veronica rinsed her face in cool
water. Next she dried her hands and
face and combed her hair.

When I Go to Church

"I'm ready to go to church now," Veronica called to her daddy. Veronica and Daddy walked down the steps of their apartment.

"Here's your Bible," Daddy said as he held her hand. "Grandmother and Grandfather are saving seats for us." Veronica and Daddy walked down the sidewalk and crossed the street to the church.

"Grandmother and I came to see the worship center," Veronica said. "We looked inside, and it is sooooo big. It's much bigger than my Sunday morning room."

"I hear the music, Daddy," Veronica said as they opened the church door. "Is the worship service starting?"

"We have a few more minutes to find seats," Daddy said. "Your grandparents want us to sit in the balcony with them."

Up, up, up. Veronica and Daddy climbed the stairs at the back of the church. Veronica could see the whole worship center from the balcony. "Big, big, big," she whispered as she looked at the zillions of seats and the red carpet and the tall ceiling.

"I see Grandmother and Grandfather," Daddy said. Veronica and Daddy walked to the front of the balcony. She grinned as she sat beside Grandmother.

Grandmother squeezed her hand, and Grandfather smiled at her.

While the music played, Veronica looked around. She saw her friend Ricardo, but he didn't see her. Next Veronica saw Mr. Bill walk to the front of the church. "Mr. Bill is the music leader," Veronica whispered to Daddy.

Veronica and Daddy stood when Mr. Bill began singing and playing his guitar. Everyone sang together. Veronica liked to hear Daddy's strong, deep voice when he sang. She hummed softly and sometimes she heard the words *friend* and *Jesus.*

They stood and sang for a long time. Veronica's legs were getting tired, but she liked hearing all of the voices singing together to make a big sound.

When they sat down, the lights began getting dimmer. Then a bright light lit the front of the church.

"Tonight, Pastor Ward is baptizing several people," Daddy whispered to Veronica.

Veronica watched as Pastor Ward helped a tall girl into the pool of water. She was wearing a white robe. Veronica listened as

Pastor Ward said, "Amelia has made an important decision and has accepted Jesus as her Savior."

Pastor Ward held onto the girl's hands as he lowered her into the water. Then he lifted her head up out of the water. After Pastor Ward baptized several people, everyone sang a song while men began passing plates for the offering.

Daddy gave Veronica several quarters to put in the offering plate. Plink—plunk—plink. Veronica's coins made a soft sound when she dropped them into the plate.

Later, Veronica listened to some of Pastor Ward's sermon as he preached.

"Why did those people go into that water?" she whispered to Daddy.

Daddy smiled and gave her a pad of paper and a pencil. "You can draw some things you saw, and we'll talk about the baptism later," he said.

Veronica drew several pictures. The pencil made scritchy—scratchy—scritchy noises on the paper.

After the sermon and a song, she put the pictures inside her Bible to take home. She stood for the prayer. Then she shook hands with people standing around her.

"I'm glad to see you here, Veronica," Amelia's mother said. Veronica and Amelia shook hands. They giggled when Grandmother hugged them both.

When I Go to Church

As Daddy and Veronica walked home, Daddy talked more about the baptism. "You're big enough to go to worship service, Veronica. Someday you'll be big enough to understand much more about baptism. We can talk about it again soon. I'm happy that you are learning."

Veronica yawned and smiled a big smile. She was tired, but happy. Sitting in church with her daddy was fun. And tonight was special because church friends were baptized. She would ask Daddy more questions when she wasn't so sleepy.

Guiding Behavior During Worship Service—Part 2

Concerns about church decorum may prevent parents from feeling free to bring their older preschoolers to worship service. What kind of behavior is "normal" for a 4- or 5-year-old and how can you respond?

- She moves around quite a bit. A preschooler's developing muscles require wiggle room. Give your child freedom to move around in a small space beside you.

- She forgets to whisper. She talks loudly sometimes. Gently remind your child to whisper when she forgets.

- She stares at other people. Much of a child's time is devoted to watching people and activities. Preschoolers do not stare to be rude; they stare because they are learners. Gently redirect your child's attention to another interest, if needed.

- She falls asleep. Try to keep your child occupied and interested. If she takes a short catnap while leaning against you, accept this need.

- She wants to leave for a drink or the rest room. Always take care of these two needs prior to the service. Encourage your child to wait. If the need is urgent, however, slip out to meet these needs.

- She wants to bring toys to the service. Resist this plea. Provide items for quiet activities such as her Bible, paper, pencil, a few crayons, chenille stems, or stickers. Place these items in a special tote bag to use exclusively for "big church."

Remember to express your expectations in positive ways. For example, say, "I'm glad you like to sing in church." Ignore negative behavior when possible. Pray for patience, wisdom, joy, and gratitude for the privilege of creating happy memories and nurturing your child's spiritual growth.

Understanding How Preschoolers Learn

How does a preschooler learn during worship services? A passive "sit still and listen" mode provides very limited learning. The following methods set the stage, however, for positive learning to occur.

- **Curiosity**—This God-given characteristic drives a preschooler's interest in what happens around him. Curiosity prompts him to ask "why," "how," and "when" questions, often in rapid succession. Try to see your child's curiosity as essential to his mental and spiritual growth rather than as an annoyance or interruption during the service.

- **First-hand Experiences and Senses**—Learning is up close and personal for a young child. He must see, hear, touch, and explore things for his brain cells to connect with his environment. Therefore, you enhance Bible learning when you encourage your child to hold his Bible, turn its pages, look at the pictures, and listen to Bible verses and stories expressed during the sermon.

- **Repetition**—When your child repeats actions, songs, words, and routines during worship services, his understanding increases. His ability to focus improves because he can "connect the dots" and gains comfort in the familiarity of simple routines of worship.

- **Imitation**—Imitating adults helps your child try out and process how things are done in a congregational worship setting. Staring, so common to preschoolers, is a behavior which allows your child to observe adults who may become role models in his spiritual development.

- **Relationships with Adults**—Loving relationships undoubtedly are the most important ways a young child learns. However, encouragement and acceptance from caring adults are necessary before other positive methods of learning take root in a child's life. Emotional and social nurturing are foundational for spiritual growth.

Baptism and Other Special Activities

Baptism, the Lord's Supper, and other special activities are occasions for explaining new words and spiritual concepts. A preschooler's natural curiosity will pique her interest. The impact of these events often is underscored by the "drama" of the music, lighting, and the number of participants.

When your child asks questions about baptism:

- Whisper a brief answer, but tell her that you will talk about it again after church. Then remember to talk with her as soon as possible.
- Answer your child's questions simply and briefly. You might say: "People are baptized after they accept Jesus as their Savior. They ask Jesus to forgive their sins, and they trust Jesus to help them live for God."
- Pray for wisdom as you respond to further questions. If she wants to know when she can be baptized, you might tell her: "You are growing and learning. We can talk anytime you have questions. One day God will help us know when it is time for you to accept Jesus and be baptized."

Because your preschooler wants to feel included in the service, her interest in the Lord's Supper likely will be strong, also. Explain that the bread and juice help remind people that Jesus is their Savior. Tell her that she will be able to participate one day.

Even though these statements about baptism and the Lord's Supper are expressed simply, preschoolers usually do not fully understand many of the words, such as *accept, Savior, sins, forgive,* and *trust*. Your patience, interest, and reassurance will help your child continue to come to you and others in your church for guidance as she grows in understanding.

The Importance of Worship for Parents

Most parents agree that attending worship service is an important example to set for their children. However, participation in congregational worship also is important for the following reasons. During worship—

• God reveals Himself to individuals. Think of the times when the Holy Spirit has comforted, encouraged, convicted, directed, or inspired you during a worship service. Worship is your invitation to God to speak to you.

• God reveals Himself to the body of worshipers. You, your family, and others present in a service corporately may enjoy oneness of spirit through the unity of God's presence and love.

• God calls His people to service. Teamwork, cooperation, sacrifice, and service often are commitments God inspires during worship. Can you recall worship services when God strengthened your resolve to extend yourself to others in ministry and service?

• You respond to God. Worship is the avenue through which you adore, exalt, and praise God. Worship is an attitude and an act of humility as you bow before God, acknowledge His sovereignty, and accept His kingship.

• You actively participate. Being a spectator is not enough. As you sing, listen, pray, and give your time and money, you perform acts that are personal investments in the worship experience. Peace, security, forgiveness, love, and other spiritual resources are replenished during genuine worship; and this influences your effectiveness as a person and as a parent.

Therefore, which is more important: attention to worship or attention to your child during worship? Because you are laying critical foundations in your preschooler's life, your attention to nurturing your child during worship services takes priority for the present. Be assured that God will bless you in this task and nurture you in the process!

Conference Plan and Study Guide for Parents

Provide a one-hour orientation for parents of preschoolers. As an alternative, parents may use the discussion questions as a personal study guide at home. A training time, however, permits parents to interact in sharing personal concerns and allows church leaders to offer encouragement and support.

Conference Plan for Guiding Preschoolers in Congregational Worship

Before the Session

- Publicize the conference and invite parents of preschoolers and church leaders.
- Post the conference name outside the meeting room door.
- Arrange seating in groups of three to six chairs.
- Provide a table and materials at the door for parents to make name tags (first names only).
- Provide copies of the discussion questions and place these in each chair. (On the handout, provide space under each question for conferees to write answers.)
- Request that parents bring copies of the book, *When I Go to Church: Guiding Preschoolers in Worship*. Provide at least two additional copies for each discussion group.
- Drape a table with a colorful cloth and display the following items: the book *When I Go to Church;* the Read to Me Bible for Kids (Holman); several construction paper Bible markers; a church bulletin; an offering plate containing a dollar bill and several quarters; and a cloth "going to church" bag containing paper, crayons, stickers, a Bible, and a lacing card and yarn.
- Attach to the walls posters with these verses:
  * *I rejoiced with those who said to me, "Let us go to the house of the Lord." Psalm 122:1*
  * *Whoever welcomes one child … in My name welcomes me. Matthew 18:5*
  * *Teach a youth about the way he should go; even when he is old he will not depart from it. Proverbs 22:6*
- Provide a CD player and CD of music from a church service.

During the Session

- Begin and close the session on time.
- Play the CD music quietly as conferees arrive and during small group work.
- Welcome conferees at the door and assist them with name tags and seating.
- Begin the session with prayer.
- Introduce yourself and other church leaders.
- Invite conferees to share aloud words or short phrases that describe congregational worship.
- Direct attention to the handout (provided in each chair) and ask conferees to form small groups. Assign each group one of the eight discussion questions on the handout. (Depending on the number of groups, you might need to assign each group more than one question.)
- Instruct each group to choose one person who will briefly summarize their small group's insights following several minutes of group work and discussion. Distribute extra copies of the book *When I Go to Church* as needed.
- Call for group reports, encouraging conferees to focus on the areas of interest and concern. (Allow an average of 3-4 minutes for each of the discussion questions.)

- Direct attention to items on the display table as they relate to the discussion (particularly the Read to Me Bible for Kids and the "going to church" bag and its contents).
- Collect the copies you provided of the book *When I Go to Church* following group discussions.
- Invite a volunteer to choose and read aloud one of the verses printed on wall the posters.
- Ask a church leader to close with a prayer for God's blessing on parents and preschoolers.

Bonus Activity

Invite parents to make simple lacing cards to include in a "going to church" bag for their child if time permits (or if parents wish to remain after the session for the activity).

Provide these items: Bible story pictures (from outdated Sunday School leader packs), scissors, large index cards, glue sticks, hole punches, yarn.

Instruct parents to select pictures to trim and glue onto index cards, punch holes around the perimeter of the picture cards, and tie a length of lacing yarn onto each card. Tell parents that a Bible picture-lacing card is a quiet activity their preschoolers may enjoy during a worship service.

Discussion Questions for Guiding Preschoolers in Congregational Worship

(May Be Used as a Personal Study Guide)

1. What are some aspects of worship from the adult perspective and from the perspective of a preschooler? (See pages 24 and 47.)

2. What kind of worship experiences for a child can occur in the home? (See page 14.)

3. What should parents keep in mind as they choose and use a Bible for their preschoolers? (See page 14.)

4. What can parents do during the week and on Sunday morning to prepare a child for worship service? (See pages 14, 15, 24, and 34.)

5. What are some positive benefits from taking a preschooler for an informal tour of the worship center? (See page 25.)

6. What are some examples of positive guidance and how is it used with preschoolers in a worship service? (See pages 34, 35, and 44.)

7. What are some of the various ways preschoolers learn? (See page 45.)

8. How can church leaders and church members help parents and preschoolers participate in congregational worship? (See pages 5, 24, 25, and 45.)